ON THE ENFORCEMENT OF
LAW IN CITIES

PATTERSON SMITH REPRINT SERIES IN
CRIMINOLOGY, LAW ENFORCEMENT, AND SOCIAL PROBLEMS

A listing of publications in the SERIES *will be found at rear of volume*

PUBLICATION NO. 74: PATTERSON SMITH REPRINT SERIES IN
CRIMINOLOGY, LAW ENFORCEMENT, AND SOCIAL PROBLEMS

ON THE
ENFORCEMENT OF
LAW IN CITIES

By

BRAND WHITLOCK

Montclair, New Jersey

PATTERSON SMITH

1969

SBN 87585-074-X

Library of Congress Catalog Card Number: 69-14952

An Open Letter Addressed to

MESSRS. JULIUS J. LAMSON, M. J. RIGGS, L. V. McKESSON
F. B. RESPESS, L. E. CLARK, HENRY C. TRUESDALL,
HERBERT P. WHITNEY AND KARL A. FLICK-
INGER, REPRESENTATIVES OF THE FED-
ERATION OF CHURCHES, TOLEDO

NOTE

When this letter was written a few thousand copies were printed in pamphlet form for local distribution, but the general demand has been so great and so surprising that another and larger edition has been found necessary. It is, of course, gratifying that this is so, especially as it gives opportunity to say that since the first edition of the letter I have been informed that the idea concerning the relation of poverty and drunkenness was expressed many years ago by Miss Francès E. Willard, founder of The Woman's Christian Temperance Union, in a letter to Mr. Stoughton Cooley of Chicago. Miss Willard's statement was to the effect that drunkenness is more frequently caused by poverty than poverty by drunkenness. I regret that I did not have it at the time the letter was written, but as with most letters and most speeches, the best things occur to one after the performance.

B. W.

25 May, 1910.

ON THE ENFORCEMENT OF
LAW IN CITIES

ON THE ENFORCEMENT OF LAW IN CITIES

Gentlemen: When recently you called upon me with a statement of your views of certain phases of the morals of the town, including suggestions as to how those morals might be improved by me, I told you that I would consider your words and communicate with you. I have considered them and I now reply.

The subject that you introduce is large, and I wish it appeared as simple to me as it seems to appear to some. It is a subject as old as humanity, as old as the fact of human sin, and to understand it, to discuss it properly or fully, would require a profound knowledge of the psychology and of the environment, social, political, and economic, of all peoples in all times. I had thought and read and studied and even made bold to write and speak on

these subjects before I became mayor, and since I became mayor I have pondered them still more deeply. I have tried to discover my duty. This, which perhaps seems an easy thing to those who have never had the responsibility, is nevertheless not quite easy, after all.

I recognize, I assure you, the sincerity of your desire to improve conditions in this city, and in that respect we have a common aim, which is to make Toledo a better city to live in, to provide here a cleaner, wholesomer environment for all people, and to uplift and improve the common lot. The methods which, as it appears to me, are best calculated to bring this end to pass, I hope to make clear in this letter. I should count myself fortunate if I could have your assistance in the work I am trying to do, for I believe that therein lies the best, perhaps the only hope of success in what you are trying to do. What I am trying to do, in my personal and official capacity—and I do not believe that a man can so dualize his personality as to do in one what he would not in the other—

2

is to aid in that vast and noble movement toward the people, which, to me, is the most inspiring expression of the yearnings of humanity to-day. This is the movement toward democracy, toward that condition in which the ideals of America, and indeed the ideals of lovers of humanity in all ages, shall be realized. This would mean a nation of free men, it would mean a city of free men, men freed from the bondages which you see enslaving them, men freed from the bondages which I see enslaving them.

What you regret and deplore and what I regret and deplore, is the existence of vice and crime in the world to-day. You propose to abolish them by the use of force; in my philosophy they can never be abolished until we ascertain the causes of them, and then remove those causes. To do this, we shall have to undertake reforms with which the policemen and the jailer will have little to do; indeed, the accomplishment of those reforms will do away with the policemen and the jailer, or release them from their present duties of destruction, to real service

for mankind. These reforms should eventually do away with those influences in our system which give monopolies and privileges to a few, and by denying common rights to the many, reduce them to a condition of involuntary poverty. For it is involuntary poverty, and its direct and indirect effects, that produce crime, and our duty is to make involuntary poverty impossible. To do this we must do away with monopoly and with privilege, and this, as I fully recognize, is a tremendous task, for there are far more monopolies, far more privileges than many suppose. But with these privileges done away, every one will have a chance to do good and to be good, and then, and not until then, will the condition which we all desire come to pass. In other words, I am doing what I can, and that I know is very little, to abolish not merely the symptoms, but the causes of involuntary poverty, which is, as I see it, to stop the source of evil and crime and vice. In the discharge of the duties of the office I hold, I have tried to keep this ideal ever in view; what I do is done in the hope of attaining that end, what

4

I forbear to do is forborne in the hope of attaining that end. I have tried not to turn aside from the greater, the causal evil, to devote my time and energies to a pursuit of the lesser or consequent evils; I have tried not to overlook the cause in contemplating the effect. This much, in the outset, I think it is due to me that you realize and understand.

It is small wonder that exaggerated ideas of conditions in Toledo should obtain, because, when the activities of Mayor Jones on behalf of the people began years ago to menace privilege in this town, privilege did what it always does when pursued, namely, it sought to distract attention from itself by seeking to raise other issues. And when this failed, it began through its various voices, persistently and systematically, to traduce the character of the city. This effort, which did, perhaps, influence certain well-meaning persons, had for its object, not the good of the people, but rather their spoliation, and, indeed, the perpetuation and extension of the very forces which produce the evils then alleged. This effort has been exerted in order that

the people might be induced to deliver over the city into the hands of those who desire privileges. They have sought to divert attention from themselves and their large immoralities to the smaller offender —an old device, always, in the hope of escape, inspired by privilege when pursued, just as friends of the fox might turn aside the hounds by drawing the aniseed bag across the trail. From such actions, inspired by such motives, it is of course idle to expect results in improved morals. Men do not gather grapes of thorn trees, nor figs from thistles, and moral improvement can never be wrought by profane methods. It would, indeed, be difficult to imagine a worse influence on the morals of a community, or a body of actions more debased or debasing, more evil in themselves, than the cowardly and indiscriminate slander of one's own city, and the wise and prudent can not fail to note, indeed, have noted, with regret that those of whom, because of their wider opportunity of enlightenment, so much better and nobler things might have been demanded, have not shown as much civic spirit, so

much concern for the common weal, as have those of smaller opportunity of whom less would naturally have been expected.

Nor is it strange that there should exist exaggerated ideas of the powers and responsibilities of the mayor for there is, singularly, an impression abroad in many minds that the mayor, by virtue of his office, possesses some peculiar occult power by which he can make people good. You and I know, of course, that this is not the case. We know that a mayor has no magic wand that he can wave over the city and make it good, and that he has no means of forcing people to be good. And indeed my conception of a mayor's duty is that no such thing is required of him. I, for instance, am not the beadle of a New England village in the year 1692, but the mayor of a modern American city in the year 1910, elected not to govern the people, but to represent them, not to bear rule over them, but to carry their will into effect. It is a convenient device, growing naturally out of an old tendency of human nature, to lay responsibility

upon others, and in the matter of morals the mayor seems to have been the one most convenient to blame. And while I regret the evil that exists and have been doing all that I can to prevent it and to substitute good for it in all ways within my power, if the responsibility is to be laid wholly upon me, I assure you that such a reliance must fail. Men are not made good by legal declaration, or by official action; they are not good because of the fear of policemen or of the pains and penalties of the laws. They are good when they follow the best and highest impulses of their souls; goodness is developed from within, and there is no other way by which any one can become good. There are, I think, after all, very few, if any, really bad persons in the world. There are those who do bad things at times, and, in common with all of us, commit many human blunders, follies and mistakes. I think that much of what we call badness arises out of conditions for which the individual is not responsible, that men are good largely as they have the chance and the incentive to be good, and that it

is our duty to see to it that all men have this chance and this incentive multiplied more and more. The responsibility for the conditions which we all deplore, therefore, can not rest solely upon any one person, even though he be an official; it rests upon all, and if we could recognize this fact, and each do his part to improve conditions, it would not be long before a genuine uplift would be felt. This can best be brought about, I think, by seeking out the causes of vice and crime, and then by removing those causes. This would be a large task, but it is a task which should be undertaken, a task which, I believe, mankind must ere long undertake if we as a people, as a city, as a state and as a nation, are to advance.

In the face of all this exaggeration, however, and despite the slander of the city, the fact fortunately remains that the people of Toledo are peaceable; they love and maintain order. While here as elsewhere, there are, of course, violations of law and many conditions which we wish were otherwise, the people as a whole are as law-observ-

ing as any that can be found, and I assert that there is no city, no municipality, great or small, in Ohio, in America, or in all the world, in which the people as a whole are better or more moral than in Toledo. A certain delicacy might have deterred me from mentioning the fact that they had recently elected me to the office of mayor, but since you say that you "feel the more willing to address me upon this subject" because the people have recently elected me "to the office of mayor with larger authority and responsibility for the enforcement of these laws," and thus have introduced the subject, I may be pardoned for saying that—since the same complaints which you now make were made in the recent municipal campaign, as they have been made in all municipal campaigns for a decade, and that in spite of them the people had again, for the third time, chosen me for this office— it might be a not unwarrantable assumption that the people were satisfied upon these points and with the manner in which I had exercised the powers and met the responsibilities of my office. Had they not

10

been satisfied it might be assumed that they would have needed the advice so freely given and selected some of the other candidates proposed for this position. But I did not wish to speak of that and I do not care to press the point.

What I had in mind to say was that when the people elected me to the office of mayor again last fall there was no larger authority or responsibility for the enforcement of law than there had been before. It is true that by a recent amendment to the municipal code known as the Paine law, the authority of the mayor and his powers and responsibilities were indeed largely increased, with reference, however, to but one department of the city government. Heretofore the administrative functions of the municipal government,—all those relating to public works; that is to the streets, water-works, harbors, bridges, sidewalks, cemeteries, houses of correction, etc.,— were vested in an elective board of public service, but by the Paine law the board of public service was abolished and for it there has been substituted a director of public service appointed by the mayor.

This has the effect of making the mayor ultimately responsible for the administration of the department of public service, or public works, but otherwise excepting only as the elimination of the board of public safety makes for concentration and mobility his powers remain what they were with reference to the enforcement of law and to any influence he may have upon the morals of the people. The duties of the mayor with respect to the enforcement of law were defined long ago, and under these new amendments remain what they have been. Section 129 of the Municipal Code (Sec. 4250 and 4548 N. R. S.) says that the mayor "shall be the chief conservator of the peace within the corporation." Section 1746 of the Revised Statutes (Sec. 4248 N. R. S.) says that the mayor "shall perform all duties prescribed by the by-laws and ordinances of the corporation, and it shall be his special duty to see that all ordinances, by-laws and resolutions of the council are faithfully obeyed and enforced." Section 4549 N. R. S. confers upon the mayor within the cor-

porate limits the same power that the sheriff has "to suppress disorder and keep the peace." These three sections constitute the whole body of the law upon that aspect of a mayor's duty. The oath of office taken by a mayor, so frequently referred to in perfervid discussion, or, as in my case, the affirmation he makes, obliges him to support the constitution and to discharge the duties of the office faithfully, honestly and impartially.

It will be seen that the three statutes I have just cited, like some other enactments, are not exactly of crystalline clearness, and that they do not define a mayor's duties with that precision and particularity that some have imagined. It is clear that the mayor is to enforce the city ordinances, that he is to maintain the public peace and that he possesses, in his quality of conservator, the magisterial powers of a justice of the peace. He is not required, as I have said, to be a beadle, or a public mentor, or a censor of the morals, acts and opinions of other people; nor is he to constitute himself a spy, and to go peeping and prying about

after violations of law. Without undertaking a lengthy discussion of his duties, I presume it may fairly and reasonably be said that so long as a mayor does his best, according to his powers, his conscience, the instrumentalities provided him, and the state of public opinion, to preserve the peace, to enforce the city ordinances, and to suppress public disorder, he is doing what the law requires. There are other officials, of course, charged with the duty of executing the laws, such as the judges, prosecuting attorneys, the sheriff, etc., and there are others who, like the mayor, are conservators of the peace, and while I realize that it is desired to confine this discussion to me, I can not resist the impulse to say that I have often wondered why these other officials have been so completely ignored in the discussions of these subjects with which Toledo is so frequently enlightened. Fortunately, the peace of this city has not for years been seriously menaced or violated and this probably is due not so much to the laws, or to the efficiency of conservators and other officials or to the presence or

14

fear of policemen, as it is to the fact that the people are industrious and peaceably inclined and have no desire to engage in brawls or disturbances or to commit breaches of the peace.

In addition to all this, my duty, according to the fundamental principles of our governmental system, consists, as I understand it, in carrying out the will of the people of this city, not the best people alone, not the wisest people alone, not the good people alone, whoever they are, not the people of any one class. This includes, theoretically, those who were opposed to my being mayor as well as those who were in favor of my being mayor; it includes the bad, whoever they are, and the poor, and all the rest. This is the theory, though of course, practically, I can not carry out the will of every man and woman. I might say, as Carlyle once said, that I have many judges, or, as the old proverb puts it, "He that builds by the wayside has many masters." There are here in Toledo nearly 200,-000 persons, of different tongues, races, creeds, interests, needs, traditions, ideals, views of what is

good and what is bad, what is right and what is wrong, what is wise and what is foolish, what is expedient and what is inexpedient. They differ on all these points; each has his own notion of how I should act, each his own conception of my duty, according to his tradition, employment, education, environment, economic condition, etc. They all differ in these respects, they differ in large divisions and classes, differ in everything perhaps except in the great fact of their common brotherhood in humanity—the one preeminent fact unfortunately ignored by men. Even you of this committee, who are agreed on certain points perhaps would not agree on all points touching my duty; how then do you think the matter stands with a whole densely packed population, dwelling together on a few square miles of land, speaking a score of tongues and with all those curious and inscrutable differences that mark a cosmopolitan population?

There are, to be sure, on the scrolls of the state, and on the books of the city, statutes and ordinances which forbid the commission of certain sins, and

even enlarge venial offenses to the proportions of crimes for the sake of prohibiting them, and having enacted this legislation society seems to be content because a theoretical remedy has been provided against evil. All that remains, according to the theory, is to "enforce" these statutes and ordinances, and the evils will vanish, the sins cease. But these remedies are theoretical only. They do not, as I have said, search out the mysterious and obscure causes of crime; they are concerned solely with the symptoms or surface indications of those deeply hidden causes. But, however that may be, these statutes and ordinances can be administered only by human agencies, and in their administration are encountered human obstacles.

It is easy to utter words and to employ phrases, such as "law enforcement," etc. In what does the "enforcement" of a law or statute consist? It consists, according to one opinion, in the following: In a city there is a man, called a mayor because he has been voted into an office by a majority of the people; there is another man called a director

of public safety, chosen by the mayor; there is still another man, called a chief of police, selected in a different manner, and there are still others, more numerous, selected in still another way, called policemen, who wear garments of a certain color, fashioned in a certain but uniform manner, and fastened by gilt buttons. There are still others, called officials, each with his distinct title, such as judge of the police court, turnkeys, superintendent of the house of correction, guards, jailers, etc. All of these men, though called officials, are nevertheless men, and the only real distinction between them and other men is that they have what is called "authority," that is, there are those called subordinates, who do what they are told to do. Thus the mayor tells the director of public safety to enforce a law, whereupon the director of public safety tells the chief of police to enforce a law, and then the chief of police tells the policemen to enforce a law. The policemen thereupon, seeing an individual violating that law, or hearing that he has violated it, seize him, lead him before the judge, tell the judge that

18

he has violated the law, and the judge tells other men, called by different titles, to take the man to the house of correction, and there deliver him, with a paper on which there are certain written directions and the impression of a seal, to a prison keeper, who is to lock the man up for a certain number of days. This process is what is called "enforcing a law," and it is supposed that by it the man who violated the law will be prevented from violating it again and that other men, who have been thinking of violating it, or intend to violate it, will be deterred from doing so and that still other men, who are bad, or are about to become bad, will be kept good. It is considered and believed that this will be the effect, because it has been so stated and written and printed in books.

Now, whenever the act in which the violation of that law consists is one which the majority of the people do not want to commit, and think it wrong to commit, an act *malum in se*, as the lawyers say, that is, one in and of itself immoral, and so condemned by the universal conscience of mankind, then

it is comparatively easy to go through with this process. But when the act which violates that law is venial, and *malum prohibitum* and would not be wrong in itself, when large numbers of the people, or a majority of the people wish to commit that act or have no objection to others committing it,—such an act, for instance, as playing ball, going to a theater, drinking beer, trimming a window, running a train, or having ice-cream delivered for the Sunday dinner, then it becomes a difficult matter to carry out such a process, and it becomes impossible to carry out such a process without resorting to violence, namely, by rushing policemen here and there in patrol wagons, and forcibly carrying away men and women to police stations, courts and prisons, and when they are out, doing the same thing over again. This process, when attempted on a large scale, is called a "crusade," is invariably accompanied by disorder and tumult, sometimes by riot, and always engenders hatred and bad feeling. Its results are harmful, and it being found to be

impossible to sustain the high pitch of excitement and even hysteria which are necessary to conduct a crusade properly, that is, according to the precedents, as it should be conducted, the enthusiasm of crusading officials soon subsides, other duties are found to demand attention, and so the crusade dies out, is abandoned, and things are worse than before.

Such a method I have not considered it advisable to adopt. It has been tried, here and elsewhere, again and again, and invariably has failed. It produces no permanent good, and is often more demoralizing than the conditions it seeks to remedy. It chokes the court with cases accumulated by a resort to those dilatory processes of the law devised and intended to safeguard the innocent, and its sporadic character and sensational features but attract attention to the evil instead of to the good, and expose, in a manner out of all relation and proportion, conditions which exist in all cities, and always have existed in all cities and towns; and, further-

more, by overshadowing the good qualities of the city, which are in great preponderance, it gives it an evil and sinister reputation which it does not deserve.

There is, however, another method that may be employed to enforce the laws. This consists in a determined, sincere, constant effort to correct evil conditions: first, by seeking out and wherever possible removing their causes; secondly, by steady repression and discouragement; and thirdly, by striving to create a higher concept of life and conduct. So far as relates to the police this system consists in constant repression by them of the worst and most flagrant evils of a positive character, such as wine-rooms, gambling, disorderly saloons and resorts, etc. This method is one that was adopted by this administration, the one that has been followed, the one that will continue to be followed until some better system can be devised or suggested. This plan has been carried, in many instances, to the length of placing a police officer in uniform at the door of a disorderly saloon or

house, which invariably discourages and in a short while ruins the patronage of the place. Such, I say, has been the policy of this administration.

I agree with you fully that wine-rooms, gambling, and the social evil, not only in the form in which you complain of it, namely, street-walking, but in all other forms, are indefensibly bad, and that they should be suppressed. I agree with you as to the evils of intemperance and as to all the evils that proceed from the saloon. And I have tried, by the use of the means at my command, and so far as my powers extend, to do away with them all. I have instructed the police to enforce the ordinances against them, and for that matter all the city ordinances. And when your letter came, I referred it to the director of public safety with instructions to investigate the conditions you complained of, and to do all in his power to remedy them. It will no doubt relieve you, as it did me, to learn that your information was not on all points accurate, but there was room for improvement and much of this has been wrought. What has been done, you no

doubt know already, but whether you do or not, I am warranted in saying that the wine-room has been eliminated; and more than this, that the combination saloon—if you know what that is—is being abolished; that street-walking has been done away with; that gambling, at least in those forms that are not purely social, or in accordance with business usages, has been suppressed; that the saloons close promptly at midnight, and that numerous saloons and disorderly houses have been forced to discontinue. Much of this had been accomplished before your letter was presented, some has been done since, and we shall not abate our efforts in this direction; we shall try to make conditions better. The director of public safety knows my wishes and has, and has had for months, my instructions on these points, and he will carry them out. The law is as well enforced in Toledo as it is in any large city; the moral tone of the town is as good as policemen can make it, and indeed, much better than it could be made by any kind of mere brute force.

In all these matters, however, there are difficulties which I should like to present to you, and certain reflections which I take this opportunity to express. Take for instance, the subject of the wine-room. I realize fully the evil of wine-rooms, and sincerely and profoundly deplore the fact that they have existed. And I have tried as best I know how to do away with such places. But that has not been easy. It is customary to speak of "wine-rooms" and to use the term "wine-room" as if there were a certain, definite, specific kind of place, easily identified, known to all, referred to by all and accepted by all as a "wine-room" and as such prohibited by and amenable to law. The fact is, of course, that the term "wine-room," in the local vernacular, means a saloon frequented by women as well as men. The saloon, as well as the restaurant, is a legal institution recognized by statute, and the law does not deny women the right to enter a saloon as men do or to drink there as men do, one of the few relations, by the way, in which the law regards women as equal with men. It is easily to be seen,

therefore, that it is difficult to provide legislation that shall regulate this practise and at the same time be constitutional.

Notwithstanding this fact, this is the first administration in Toledo's history that has made an effort to enact such legislation and three years ago an ordinance was passed by the council in an effort to suppress such places. The legal effect of this ordinance is to define a wine-room as a saloon or restaurant in which there are closed stalls and it makes it illegal for two persons of opposite sex to be alone together in such stall or room. I instructed the police the day the ordinance became effective to enforce it; the police have tried to enforce it and to such an extent have they succeeded that I think it may be said that there are at least no saloons in Toledo to-day that are in technical violation of that ordinance. That is to say, there are no saloons with private rooms or stalls, or if there are they are in existence without the knowledge of the police. But, of course, this does not cure the evil. There have been saloons,

possibly are saloons to-day, where women **congre-**gate with men, where they drink with men, and these places are not confined to what by some are termed the lower strata of society. The police have not been content with trying merely to enforce the ordinance, but in numerous instances where there have been disorderly saloons frequented by women and men the director of safety or the chief of police has placed an officer in uniform at the door, and it has been found that such a method has been so effective in discouraging patronage that such resorts have been forced to suspend business or else to tone down the demeanor of their patrons and patronesses to a degree more conformable with the usages of higher society.

That there are in this city, as you state, numerous wine-rooms into which boys and girls are invited, I can not believe. The police have exercised great vigilance in this matter, and are actuated by a sincere desire to prevent such atrocious practises. They are doing this. They will continue to do this. And they will continue to try to suppress wine-

rooms as well as all other disorderly places, and I think that any one who will seek to know the facts, will find that this evil has been greatly reduced in this city.

Again, when you complain of street-walking, you refer to a condition that has existed in all cities, in all countries and in all times. You bring up a problem here as old as humanity, as old as sin, and I am glad that you regard the men in this respect as being as bad as the women. And you present one phase of a problem which I confess at the very outset I can not solve, one which I venture to say no man could solve even if he were in my position. The social evil is one with which public officials have contended for ages. It is one which has been made the subject of countless laws, from the time of the Mosaic code, down to the latest revision of the statutes. It has been the basis of the speculations of moralists, philosophers and sociologists. It is a subject upon which the prophets of old uttered their inspired moralities. But the scarlet woman has survived all manner of edicts and decrees and

whole folios of impotent legislation. She has been made the subject of a dramatic period in one of the imperishable orations of Cato in the Roman Senate. She has evoked one of the most eloquent passages of the famous historian of European morals whose imaginative vision could behold her, while creeds and civilizations rise and fall, the eternal priestess of humanity, blasted for the sins of the people. And the pathetic figure remains, to typify a sad, age-old problem that is seemingly as insoluble as ever.

The social evil presents itself in cities in three principal phases: first—I must speak plainly—that of the brothel; secondly, street-walkers; thirdly, women who are supported, often in luxurious surroundings, by paramours. Of this last class we do not speak. Society does little more than lift her brows on that phase, and the law there does not interfere any more than it interferes with other prostitutions quite as deplorable, quite as sickening, and far more reprehensible because they are wholly without excuse, namely, those of lawyers and clergy-

men and artists and writers and speakers prostitut-
ing their talents in the service of the privileged
classes of society for the sake of their favor, their
patronage or their reward.

What you speak of is the second class, the street-
walkers. Now there are ordinances which prohibit this kind of soliciting on the street and there
are ordinances which prohibit what is known as
loitering on the street. The last offense is one
very loosely defined, the enactment is liable to
much abuse and, as many lawyers assert, is probably without constitutional validity. Laws seeking to regulate, diminish, or extirpate the social
evil have been confined almost exclusively to the female. Since the days of Aholah and Aholibah, the
man has been guiltless, but the woman has borne
her iniquity, and it is only recently that there has
been anything like an acceptance of the truth that
there should be an equal standard of morals for men
and women. It would be difficult, even for a man
possessed of that wide discretion and deep per-
spicacity which inhere in policemen the moment

they get a blue coat on their backs, and a shield on their breasts, to detect among women on the street at night, those that were of ill-repute; and it would be still more difficult for them to tell whether the men on the streets at nights were, as you say, unprincipled or not. I think it would be very dangerous to make them thus the silent and irresponsible judges of the motives and morals of people they meet. So we see at once that in this particular application the doctrine is exceedingly delicate, and about all the police can do is to drive from the streets those women who are known to be common prostitutes. And they might arrest men who were insulting females, although it is difficult, because of the modesty of women—some shreds remaining even to the most unfortunate—to secure convictions in this class of cases. Yet this is exactly what the police have been doing, and are doing all the time. Policemen have been detailed in the down-town districts at night and they have been striving to keep these women off the streets and they do this by my orders. And I believe that, as a result of that

policy, as I have said, and as the reports show, the down-town streets are free from this condition.

Do you know that when I said that this had been done by my orders I did not experience any sense of personal elation or satisfaction? The law was responsible, to be sure, but a man does not like to make war on women. Having been driven from the streets, where are these women to go? Are they to be driven out of town? That would be only to transfer the problem to some other locality. They can not be driven into the river, or put to death, at least any faster than society already drives them into the river or to death. Who will take them? At whose door will they knock for shelter? At whose establishment shall they apply for employment? What are they to do? I'll tell you; they can go either to the river or to the brothel. In either case has the situation been improved? If they select the brothel, their own moral condition certainly has not been advanced, and I doubt much if the general tone of society has been raised. About the only advantage gained is that the calm breasts

of the good men who walk the streets are no longer to be agitated, and a visible temptation has been removed from the young. It seems indeed, and I think that you, as men of affairs, have faced this conclusion, that the modern municipality must take its choice. It may drive these women off the streets and into the house with the red light, or it may drive them out of the house into the white light of the street at night. We here are trying to keep these women off the streets. But the condition of these women is to me so abject, so pitiable, and so sad that I have no relish in such work. Somehow the sins of others, the mistakes and the failures of others, can not excite in me that moral indignation which exists in the breasts of some, nor can it in me be artificially provided by an affectation of that impersonal precision, which as it is supposed, should replace in an official all human feeling.

The only consolation I have in dealing with this question is that we have a chief of police who has a big heart and has done much good, about the only good, I think, that I ever knew an official of the law

to do these poor people. After they have been taken to the police stations, he personally investigates each case and there are many instances in which, at his own expense, he has sent girls to their homes and restored them so far as might be to a former, better condition of life. And I think it would be worth any one's while some morning to sit with him when he is hearing these sad and sordid tales of broken lives and blasted hopes. It would stir the hardest heart to some human pity, some sympathy with the fallen.

There is much more that I might say on the subject, much that I should like to say, much that perhaps ought to be said. There is somehow an impression that these women and habitués of the tenderloin are there because they want to be there, that they lead the kind of life they do because it is happy and joyous. Some speak of it indeed, as if they themselves were deterred from adopting it only by the fear of some future deprivation or punishment, and that for the sacrifice they make here they are to be rewarded appropriately hereafter.

But the fact is that these women are in that condition not because they want to be but because they have to be, because once in it through a mistake, and generally not a mistake of their own, society will not let them seek any other condition or rise to any higher level. As the saying is and as the general belief seems to be, each with reference to himself at any rate, they "have to live." How are they to live in our civilization unless they can get money? And how are they to get money unless they can get a job? And what job is open to them other than the one they have? So long as women are kept economically dependent on men, just so long will this condition exist, just so long will officials and administrations and society have to choose one or the other horn of this dilemma. And until the dawning of a better day in which there shall be equal opportunity for men and women, equal opportunity to find employment and to earn money and to keep what they make, just so long will this class of poor creatures exist in our communities. If a man falls he does not lose his job or his position

in society or his chance of life, and so economically that fact does not drive him either to the river or to the brothel or to the tenderloin or to walk the streets at night to get his bread. In the eyes of society or in the conditions of our civilization it affects him little, however much it may affect him in his own character.

But there is another branch of this subject. Many girls who find themselves compelled to make a living are confronted with the impossibility of making that living because the wages paid are too small to live upon. And herein the employer who is grasping profits has a certain responsibility, and while he may evade that responsibility in his own mind or in the minds of others by complaining of the mayor or of the police, I do not think he will be able to evade that responsibility when he faces that God to whom he prays. The recent report of the government on the so-called white slave traffic shows the effect of this cause and bears out a statement of the eminent authority, Doctor Sanger, who in his book, *The History of Prostitution*, says:

"A prolific cause of female depravity can be found in the several tables, showing the description of the employment pursued and the wages received by the women previous to their fall, and it will be a question for the political economist to decide how far mere business consideration should be an apology on the part of employers for a reduction in their rates of remuneration, and whether the savings of a small percentage in wages is not more than counterbalanced by the enormous amount of taxation enforced on the public at large to defray the expenses incurred on account of a system of vice, which is the direct result in many cases of insufficient compensation for honest labor."

And then there is the more indirect but no less potent effect of the manipulation that goes on under the form of law in our country, that subtle process of exploitation and appropriation which makes millionaires of a few and paupers and criminals of many. In the first cold days of winter, the monopolist may raise the price of meat or bread or oil, and in a lordly way give the proceeds of his

facile extortion to charity, and at the same moment and because of what he has done, somewhere in these big cities of ours, some poor girl succumbs and goes out on the streets to get her bread.

And when we reflect that these women are but women after all, that like their more fortunate sisters, they like comfort and fine clothes, it will be seen, I trust, that they are not to be condemned altogether and eternally if, in their desire to have these things which they see other women in economic ease and security enjoying to the point of luxury and extravagance, they yield to the temptations everywhere about them. To imagine that this condition can be cured or even bettered by the brutalities of prisons, after they have been tried for thousands of years and by all are admitted to have failed, and failed miserably, is absurd. Such methods have no tendency other than to brutalize and embitter their victims, and all the serious students of this subject, all the criminologists, Doctor Alfred Blaschko, Havelock Ellis, and the rest, are agreed that legal restrictions and moral crusades have never influ-

enced conditions in the least. We shall never solve this problem by pretending an outraged morality, nor by hounding the prostitute; we shall never solve it until we open our eyes and see that it is merely one of the many evils of industrial slavery and legal privilege.

I might refer to another aspect of this problem and by it show that these same women of ill-repute have, nevertheless, an important part in our civilization and in our society. If one will trace just where the money goes which they make at such dreadful sacrifice of body and of soul, if one will think of the exorbitant rents that are charged for those squalid tenements in which they lead those lives which seem to impress some as being so happy and luxurious, and reflect that there are gentlemen who are respected and count themselves among the good and eminent of the town, who own the property where these poor creatures dwell, one will have some deeper reflections and indeed some deeper perplexities upon this subject. We have had in this town quite recently an example of the very practical

manner in which economic changes may effect what are called moral conditions. The board of assessors of real property the other day raised the valuation of realty in that portion of the city called the tenderloin, that is, the board wisely assessed it according to its earning power. We all know the sinister implications of the phrase "earning power" in this relation; we all know what it connotes, we all know its vast implications. And no action taken by the police or by the criminal courts could have the influence for good that this blow struck at the root will have; this very practical method of rendering vice unprofitable, not to its immediate practitioners, for they suffer now from it, but to the ultimate recipients of its profits, those higher up in society, to whom all this vice ministers and whom it supports. I do not wish, however, to be understood as blaming particularly those who rent places for this purpose. I should be disposed to blame them more, if I blamed them at all, for their public protestation than for their participation in the business, for they, too, are but the impotent victims of

40

our social system; they can be released from its
difficulties, from its pains and from its insidious
influences for evil only when all men are released
from it. This social system, with privileges for
the few, and proscription for the many, creates
these conditions and these types, and we can not
get rid of either, no matter what we do, so long
as we continue to produce them. If the director
of public safety were to order the police to drive
these habitués into some other town or into the river,
their places would be promptly filled the very next
day by others exactly like them. I think this fact
will become clear and patent to any one who will but
open his eyes and honestly, fearlessly, look about
him. He should be warned, however, before looking that the spectacle he is about to behold will
reveal society to him in a new light; a light which
will make him inexpressibly sad and seriously interfere with his peace of mind for the rest of his
days. But it may make him wiser; it may move
him to the desire and duty of going to the fallen
in the spirit of love, the longing to help and save

them, and I believe that, presently, he will conclude that the best way to help and to save them is to begin to reconstruct society so that it shall no longer produce the conditions that condemn thousands of his fellow human beings to such a life, or to such a death, as it is pretty certain soon to be. At any rate, if he does one of these things, he will see why these people are in the tenderloin or on the way there; he will come to see that they are not there because they want to be there, but that they are there because they have to be there, because we, all of us, that is, society, put them there. It is the inequality and the denial of brotherhood resulting logically and inevitably from privilege in our laws that put them there. It is that which makes all the poverty, all the vice, all the crime in the world, the crimes of the poor and the crimes of the rich. To maintain the economic conditions which produce these effects and put these people in the tenderloin and then to turn around and berate and beat and destroy them, seems to me a bigger crime than any

they have ever committed. It passes my comprehension how any one can look at them and see how miserable, how poor, how wretched they are and then have any feeling of hatred for them, or wish to hurt them more than we have hurt them already. In one realizing their helplessness, their dumb yearning for life, they must inspire only feelings of profoundest pity.

As to gambling, by which I presume you mean those places where men gamble with the forbidden paraphernalia of the professional gambler, I have, as already said, instructed the police to suppress it and I think that they have succeeded in doing this. If there are such places they are surreptitiously conducted without the knowledge of the police authorities and if discovered will be abated. I am trying, and have tried and shall continue to try by the use of the means at my command, to continue the suppression of this evil and to put a stop to this form of gambling. That is the policy of this administration, and orders in accordance

with that policy have been issued by the director of public safety to the police, are now standing and in force, and, I believe, are being executed.

And yet, when you say that in such resorts, when they do exist, "men risk their earnings, thereby impoverishing themselves and families", I fear you do not fully realize just how our civilization works. It is not the men who earn the money, that is, the laboring men, who gamble. They are too busily employed, and, in general, too honest and too intelligent to do this sort of thing. The lives they lead, full as they are of hard work, do not offer the leisure for such dissipation. They have not been contaminated by luxury and do not have to seek, in a gratification of the senses, those forms of vice which appeal to the exploiting class. Gambling, which is just one expression of the spirit of speculation that is rife in our land, is not a vice of those who are engaged in productive toil. It is indulged in rather by those who live off the labor of others, those who do not earn money but merely gather or appropriate, often by the subtle processes

of the law, the money that has been earned by others. Gambling is essentially a vice of the idle, and exists only where there is apparent in the upper classes of society that decadence which comes with wealth and luxury, all of which are made possible by those processes of exploitation which take from the man who works and give to the man who does not work. The wages of workingmen, it may therefore be said, are indeed wasted, but not by the workingman himself; they are wasted before he gets them by those who are living idle lives on the product of his toil.

But the form of gambling to which you object is not the only one that has existed in Toledo. It is, as I have said, but one expression and it is in a sense, bad though it be, a minor expression, a somewhat feeble note of that larger spirit of speculation which animates so many in society. This spirit leads a certain few to imagine that government is made for them and their personal interest and that it should give them the privilege to exploit the labor of the many, to take from them what they produce.

It expresses itself in speculative operations in stocks and bonds and in grain and produce, just as it expresses itself in the gambling that goes on in clubs, in private homes, at the whist table, at the poker table and on the stock exchange. All of these forms of gambling are abhorrent to me, as they are to you, and I am trying as best I can to do away with them all by seeing to it that the law shall cease giving privileges to the few in the way of franchises for street railways, gas companies, electric light companies, exorbitant tariffs, exemptions and the like. These processes represent gambling on an immense and sinister scale, and are far more dangerous than any other kind. They have been pointed out over and over again and could be prevented if those who profit by them were not so powerful in our society, so influential with our government, so persistent and insidious in their demands and so successful in securing and keeping for themselves the means by which they exploit others. This is, indeed, "a condition dangerous to public morals and welfare", and while it is not now altogether in

violation of law, for the simple reason that these larger and more influential gamblers have made the laws for their own benefit and protection, it "can and should be detected and prevented."

As to the saloons, the midnight ordinance is being and will continue to be enforced strictly. And, more than this, disorderly saloons the police regulate by that effective process referred to, namely, the placing of a man in uniform at the door. In many cases by these means such saloons have either been forced to become orderly, to maintain quiet, or have been put out of business. And experience has shown that this is perhaps the most effective method that can be employed under the laws as they exist to-day. You know, of course, that saloons are not licensed in this state because the constitution prohibits it, and, that, therefore, municipal authorities have not the means which exist in other states, by revoking licenses, to regulate these resorts. The fathers, as they are called, who made the constitution seem to have been opposed to the saloon and so prohibited the state from entering

into partnership with it by licensing it, and such has been the reverence for law in this state that that constitutional provision has not been violated. Instead of collecting a certain amount of money from each saloon, and giving the proprietor a piece of paper called a "license," which would undoubtedly violate the constitutional provision, the state collects from each saloon a certain amount of money, and gives the proprietor a piece of paper called a "tax receipt." By this amazing achievement in legal sophistry, by thus making a bargain after instead of before payment, by substituting one noun for another, all parties seem to have been satisfied, reverence for the constitution remains unimpaired, and, above all, the state can continue its partnership in a business it condemns and in our pregnant modern phrase, "get the money."

I have shown that all the city ordinances bearing upon the subjects you mention—and all other city ordinances, for that matter—are being enforced; at least that we are earnestly, sincerely trying to enforce them, and succeeding to a degree beyond that

hitherto achieved in this town. Coming now to the statute in reference to Sunday closing—there being, as I shall show later, no municipal ordinance on that subject—I might say with truth, that the saloons probably obey the statutes as strictly as the generality of men or of businesses do; that in general the saloons give a formal observance to this statute, which is as much as many statutes receive, and, indeed, is more than is required in most large cities of this or other states.

But I do not wish to quibble or to be disingenuous, nor do I claim that the ideal or theoretical condition which was in the minds of those who framed this statute has been achieved. In the present divided state of public sentiment it could not be achieved, and the officials therefore must do the best they can under the circumstances. This is one of the most difficult problems with which municipal authorities have to deal and the police have enforced this statute according to the policy of administrative repression already referred to. They have earnestly tried to repress

all open violations and all indecencies, and in every instance where complaints have been made of, or attention has been drawn to, disorderly or notorious places, the police have acted promptly and many such places have been entirely suppressed. In cases where there have been disorder, or noise or music or activity or even a display of lights, officers have been posted at the door. When it is considered that at the time I came into the mayor's office there was little attempt at regulation of these evils, and when that condition is compared with the state of affairs to-day, I think it may be said that an advance has been made. Certainly the peace has been conserved, and Toledo has had quiet Sundays. This seems to meet the demands of public sentiment, and of the statute itself, as far at least as the responsibility of a conservator is involved.

But this subject warrants, I think, a more extended discussion than any of the other topics you have broached, for the reason that it raises the whole question of what is generally referred to as the problem of law enforcement in cities. There

are certain statutes intended to compel observance of the Sabbath. They were passed by state legislatures long ago in all states, and are enforced in none. If there were only one city in the country where they are not observed, the effect might be attributed to the laxity of local officials, but the fact is that they are observed and enforced in no large city for any length of time and the fact further is that where it has been attempted to enforce them such action has not had the support of the public. I have been a rather close and interested student of American municipal conditions, and I know of no city where these laws have had any but a spasmodic enforcement. I am aware that those who contend that these laws should be enforced base their faith on what seems to them to be logic. They are committed to a syllogism, and they postulate their argument thus: As a major premise, all laws should be enforced; as a minor premise, the statutes relating to Sunday observance are laws, and as a conclusion, the statutes providing for Sunday observance, therefore, should be enforced. Many speak

as if this were accepted by everybody and could not be otherwise than accepted by everybody, as if it were impossible that it should be controverted, that all are agreed on this point, and that if any one disputes it he is either hypocritical, cowardly, disingenuous or dishonest. Let us see. The first premise, that all laws should be enforced, is undoubtedly correct; the second, that the statutes relating to Sunday observance are laws, contains in it the possibilities, at least, of discussion.

We are led to inquire at this point just what a law is. I shall try to avoid any purely academic treatment of this question for I do not care to bore practical business men like yourselves and so shall not attempt any review of the several definitions that have been given by jurists and philosophers such as Demosthenes, Xenophon, Cicero, Hooker, Kant, Savigny, Austin, Hobbs, Bentham, Dernberg, Blackstone and others. A course in their writings would simply lead us to agree with Sir Frederick Pollock in the statement that, "The greater a lawyer's opportunities of knowledge have been, and the more

time he has given to the study of legal principles, the greater will be his hesitation in face of the apparently simple question, 'What is law?'" Such a discussion, while not altogether beside our purpose, is unnecessary in this place. In a monarchy the law is the will of the monarch, who used to declare that it was also the will of God. In an aristocracy, the law is the will of a select few—selected, of course, by themselves. In a democracy the law is, on theory, the will of the people or of a majority of them, though even in democracies there are continual attempts, frequently successful, to substitute for the will of the people the will of a very few of the people, who consider themselves wiser, or morally better, or in some other manner superior to other people. That is, the autocratic sentiment strongly survives, and there are those who feel that they themselves and they alone are competent to judge and to say what is best for people. When, as generally happens, their views are not accepted, they seek to impose them on the people by force—for the people's good, of course. "Man-

kind should be ruled by the good," they say, "and we are the good, and the only superlatively good among mankind." Like the elder monarchs, they say that the will of God must prevail, and when asked how that divine will is to be ascertained, they modestly say, "Ask us, and we will tell you." Or, to quote the sarcasms of Bastiat, who, in opposing the idea that mankind sustains to the legislator the relation of the clay to the potter, says, "Happily there are some men, termed legislators, upon whom Heaven has bestowed opposite tendencies [to those of mankind] not for their own sake, but for the sake of the rest of the world. Whilst mankind tends to evil, they incline to good; whilst mankind is advancing toward darkness, they are aspiring to enlightenment; whilst mankind is drawn toward vice, they are attracted by virtue. And, this granted, they demand the assistance of force, by means of which they are to substitute their own tendencies for those of the human race."

But never under any circumstances, do they prohibit the acts they themselves wish to commit. It is

just as Huckleberry Finn said of the Widow Douglas when she would not let him smoke: "And she took snuff, too; of course that was all right, because she done it herself."

And yet, there is, after all, no human force greater than this same public will, this mass intelligence, and it prevails, where it knows what it wants, even in monarchies and in aristocracies. It was upon a recognition of this fact, and the principles to be deduced from it, and by the insistence of this most tremendous of all forces, that democracies were founded, and in America the law is, in theory, the will of the people.

As we investigate this subject we inevitably come to a point where we see a distinction between a law and a statute, and while no doubt our good Mayor Jones would have been amused to find himself included among the profound jurists of the world, I think that not one of them all could have given a better definition of what law is in this country than he did when he said, as he used to say frequently: "The law in America is what the people will back

up." There are, I say, differences between laws and statutes. The statute may say anything; by political tricks, by maneuvers, by chicanery, by controlling party machines, by hiring political bosses, or by bribery it can be induced to say this or that thing, to say that one man or one set of men shall have privileges that no one else enjoys. Sometimes the statutes represent the public will, other times they do not. When they do not represent the public will, while most men would say that they should be respected and observed as laws, as no doubt they should, they are not, nevertheless, in themselves, laws. Just as there are in nature certain eternal and immutable laws, governing in the field of physics and biology, so are there laws which govern in the field of sociology. We have advanced in the discovery of these laws in the realm of physics and biology, but we have not made a similar advance in discovering the laws of sociology, that is, those laws which govern men in their human relations. And, failing to discover these laws, we have attempted to enact statutes, and some of these statutes, no doubt

56

in contravention of law, have wrought much woe and mischief and have made poverty and vice and crime in the world.

We have in the history of our country numerous examples of the difference between a statute and a law. For instance, before the Civil War a statute was enacted known as "The Fugitive Slave Law," with its several amendments, intended to operate in the Northern states. But these were not laws because they did not represent the will of the people and could not be enforced. People not only violated them, but violated them with impunity, and even in pride, and in the states, legislatures passed acts in contravention and nullification of them, called "personal liberty laws." And it was no doubt a consideration of their action that led Emerson, our great philosopher who is so much admired and so little read, to say that "good men must not obey the laws too strictly."

At this distance of time, and considering the progress of the species, men view that condition with equanimity and complacency, and few could

be found who would condemn those men who placed their faith in a higher law than human statutes. Indeed we honor them and glory in their existence.

And yet there are other examples, not so lofty in sentiment, which show this force similarly at work. A current example is found in the enactment which requires people to return for taxation their personal property at its full valuation. This is a statute that is universally violated—openly, flagrantly and admittedly. I presume that I shall run little danger of being disputed even if I should risk that form of assertion most easily disproved, namely, the general statement, and say that there is not a man in all Ohio who returns his personalty to the assessor at its full value. This is a common universal practise, so generally followed that it does not content itself with the violation of one law, but involves in each instance the infraction of another law, namely, that against false swearing. For not only does each man falsely return his personal property, but he makes oath that this false statement is true. This is the universal practise, so long followed and

58

so universally acquiesced in that it amounts to a custom in society, and operates as a law in super- session of the statute. And this is done, and not ob- jected to or complained of or even criticized. It would be a dangerous apothegm to assert that in all instances such conduct, even when universal or gen- eral, is justifiable, and I most emphatically do not wish to be understood as asserting any such thing, though I will say that this is indeed a foolish and unwise law, based upon an absurd theory of taxa- tion, and, in form, as it has been in fact, should be repealed.

What I am trying to make clear is that a statute can not be fully enforced in a community where the public sentiment is opposed to it and that where it is attempted to enforce it there oftentimes result more evil than good, more harm than benefit, and that all kinds of disorders and difficulties are brought upon us by that attempt. "Law and order" is a fine phrase, beloved by the Pharisee; law and order in- deed are loving sisters who present a beautiful spec- tacle of harmony, but statute and order are not al-

ways synonymous, nor indeed compatible. The law in any community is the will of that community and according to my reason and my conscience and my principles, I deem it my duty to be guided by the will of the people whom I represent.

But let us examine a little further into this matter of law. Inasmuch as authority frequently appeals more strongly than mere reasoning, let me refer to a book with the title of *Law: Its Origin, Growth and Function*, recently published by G. P. Putnam's Sons. This book contains a course of lectures prepared for delivery to the law school of Harvard University and it was precisely the idea that I am trying to present that the distinguished author sought to teach the youth of that respectable, conservative and conventional institution of learning. He was not a radical, or even a dreamer. He was distinctly and preeminently a conservative citizen, a distinguished gentleman, resident in New York, an ornament of the bar of his own state and of the nation, perhaps the leading corporation lawyer of our times, the late James Coolidge Carter.

And from him let me quote just a few paragraphs that I may give you the line of his argument and so support the one I am trying to make. He says (p. 14), "The thing and the only thing, sought to be affected by law is human conduct. Of course in connection with human conduct everything which directly bears upon it, including especially the nature and constitution of man, and the environment in which he is placed, becomes part of the field of fact to be studied, for these are causes constantly operating upon conduct and affecting it. * * * It may possibly be found that human conduct is in a very large degree self-regulating, and that the extent to which it can be affected by the conscious interference of man is much narrower than is commonly supposed."

He argues then, (p. 119) that "the conclusion is clear that habit and custom in each of these different conditions furnish the rules which govern human conduct," and the principal function of legislation "is to supplement and aid the operation of custom and that it can never supplant it; * * *

its own efficiency is dependent upon its conformity to habit and custom. What has governed the conduct from the beginning of time will continue to govern it to the end of time. Human nature is not likely to undergo a radical change, and, therefore, that to which we give the name of Law always has been, still is, and will forever continue to be Custom. * * * Legal writers have at all times allowed much weight to custom, viewing it as one, but only one of the *sources* of law, as if there were some governmental power standing above custom, the function of which was to pronounce judgment on the wisdom of custom, and select from it the rules it would enforce and reject the rest. * * * What then is wrapped up and concealed in the word *custom* which we so often employ? * * * That thing which has held imperious sway over the conduct of men of all races, whether savage or civilized, and in all times, can not be low, trivial, or evil. Where is the secret of its power? The simplest definition of custom is that it is the *uniformity of*

conduct of all persons under like circumstances, but this suggests the question—'What is *conduct* and what is its *cause?*' To answer this without indulging in speculation, but extending our attention to all known truths ascertained by observation, whether of the world of mind or of the external world, we must avail ourselves of the teachings of the science of Psychology. *Conduct* is some *physical movement* of the body and is invariably preceded by some thought or feeling which is its cause; and this thought or feeling is produced by some operation of surrounding things—the environment —on the *nervous* constitution. Inasmuch as the constitutions of men in the same society are similar and the environment similar, the thought must be similar and the conduct consequently similar. Hence human conduct necessarily presents itself in the form of similarity—habits and customs."

The author presents his views in a series of closely-reasoned paragraphs, thus (p. 129):

"Law *begins* as the product of the automatic ac-

tion of society, and becomes in time a cause of the continued growth and perfection of society. Society can not exist without it, or exist without producing it. *Ubi societas ibi lex.* Law, therefore, is self-created and self-existent. It is the form in which human conduct—that is, human life, presents itself under the necessary operation of the causes which govern conduct. * * * Inasmuch as conduct is necessarily controlled by previous thought, and such thought is determined by individual constitution, that is, character, and the environment, nothing can directly control conduct, which can not control both character and environment. It is not therefore, possible to *make law* by legislative action. Its utmost power is to offer a reward or threaten a punishment as a consequence of particular conduct, and thus furnish an additional motive to influence conduct. When such power is exerted to reinforce custom and prevent violations of it, it may be effectual, and rules or commands thus enacted are properly called laws; but if aimed against established custom they will be ineffectual. Law not only

can not be directly made by human action, but can not be abrogated or changed by such action."

I now present some further paragraphs from this book, which show the spirit and force of the author's reasoning and commentary:

"The *Written* Law is victorious upon paper and powerless elsewhere. The Attorney-General is sensible of the feebleness of the command resting upon him to enforce a law, the enforcement of which would send a hundred of the most eminent citizens to jail and throw the industry of the country into confusion" (p. 213).

"The popular estimate of the possibilities for good which may be realized through the enactment of law is, in my opinion, greatly exaggerated. Nothing is more attractive to the benevolent vanity of men than the notion that they can effect great improvement in society by the simple process of forbidding all wrong conduct, or conduct which they think is wrong, by law, and of enjoining all good conduct by the same means; as if men could not find out how to live until a book were placed in the

65

hands of every individual, in which the things to be done and those not to be done were clearly set down" (p. 221).

"The principal danger lies in the attempt often made to convert into crimes acts regarded by large numbers, perhaps a majority, as innocent—that is to practise what is, in fact, tyranny. While all are ready to agree that tyranny is a very mischievous thing, there is not a right understanding equally general of what tyranny is. Some think that tyranny is a fault only of despots, and can not be committed under a republican form of government; they think that the maxim that the majority must govern justifies the majority in governing as it pleases, and requires the minority to acquiesce with cheerfulness in legislation of any character, as if what is called self-government were a scheme by which different parts of the community may alternately enjoy the privilege of tyrannizing over each other. The principal evils of legal tyranny arise from the instrumentality which it employs, which is always *force*" (p. 246).

OF LAW IN CITIES

"When a law is made declaring conduct widely practised and widely regarded as innocent to be a crime, the evil consequences which arise upon attempts to enforce it are apt to be viewed as the consequences of the forbidden practise, and not of the attempt to suppress it; and it is believed that the true method of avoiding, or doing away with, these consequences is to press the efforts at enforcement with increased energy. But when a mistake has been made, its consequences can not be avoided by a more vigorous persistence in it. The best means of inculcating caution in this employment of criminal legislation is to have clearly in mind its evil consequences. The species of criminal legislation to which *sumptuary* laws belong furnishes an apt illustration of them. * * * Besides the desire of doing good, the selfish determination is formed of carrying out a purpose, and the purpose comes to seem so important that no inquiry is made concerning the means except to consider what will be most effective. It suits the judgment of some and the temper of others to convert the practises they

deem so mischievous into crimes and they think that if nothing else will prevent indulgence in them, the fear of heavy punishment will at least be effective, and indeed many think that the force of law is so great that the mere enactment of a prohibition will accompany the desired end, and all are inclined to believe that even if the laws are ineffective for the purpose for which they were enacted, they will at least do no harm. But men forget that their acts, whether in enacting and attempting to enforce written laws, or of whatever other nature, are subject to the great law of causality and will draw after them their inevitable consequences. The law when enacted will not execute itself. It requires the active interposition of man to put it in force. Evidence must be found and prosecutions set in motion, and as this is a task in which good men are commonly found to be unwilling, or too indolent, to engage voluntarily, others must be sought for who will undertake it. The spy and informer are hired, but their testimony is open to much impeachment, and is met by opposing testimony often false and per-

jured. The trials become scenes of perjury and subornation of perjury and juries find abundant excuses for rendering verdicts of acquittal or persisting in disagreements, contrary to their oaths. The whole machinery of enforcement fails, or, if it succeeds at all, it is in particular places only, while in others the law is violated with impunity. * * *

"An especially pernicious effect is that society becomes divided between the friends and the foes of repressive laws, and the opposing parties become animated with a hostility which prevents united action for purposes considered beneficial by both. Perhaps the worst of all is that the general regard and reverence for law are impaired, a consequence the mischief of which can scarcely be estimated. * * * What a spectacle is thus afforded of the impotence of man's conscious effort to overrule the silent and irresistible forces of nature! He wholly fails to gain the object in view; but objects not in view, and by no means desired, are brought about on the largest scale * * * law and its administration brought into public contempt, * * *

animosity created between different bodies of citizens, rendering them incapable of acting together for confessedly good objects!" (p. 247).

I shall conclude the quotations from Carter's great work by the following (p. 251): "I do not hesitate to say that any legislation which bears the characteristics of *tyranny*, as I have defined that term, is vicious in theory and has never yet succeeded, and never will succeed, in gaining its avowed end, or in having any other than an injurious effect; and I venture to add that if the zeal and labor which have been employed by what are called the better classes of society in efforts to enact and enforce laws repressive of liberty, had been expended in kindly and sympathetic efforts to change and elevate the thoughts and desires of those less fortunate than themselves, a benefit would have been reaped in the diminution of misery and crime which compulsory laws could never accomplish. Moral ends can never be gained except by moral means. All the advances in civilization and morality which society has thus far made are due to the cul-

tivation and development of those moral sympathies which find their activity in cooperation and mutual aid."

This same theory has been set forth, more briefly, and perhaps at a higher range of philosophic thought, by Emerson, who, in the opening paragraphs of his essay on "Politics" says:

"Republics abound in young civilians who believe that the laws make the city, that grave modifications of the policy and modes of living and employments of the population, that commerce, education and religion may be voted in or out; and that any measure, though it were absurd, may be imposed on a people if only you can get sufficient voices to make it a law. But the wise know that foolish legislation is a rope of sand which perishes in the twisting; that the State must follow and not lead the character and progress of the citizen; the strongest usurper is quickly got rid of; and they only who build on Ideas, build for eternity; and that form of government which prevails is the expression of what cultivation exists in the population

71

which permits it. The law is only a memorandum. We are superstitious, and esteem the statute somewhat; so much life as it has in the character of living men is its force."

It is difficult to resist the temptation to quote at greater length, and from other writers on this subject, but I must forbear. I trust, however, that enough has been said to set forth this theory, and therefore, I shall pass to the practical application of it to our present situation.

Bearing in mind, then, the distinction between a law and a statute, we find that the basis of the statute for Sunday closing of saloons, is not, as will be at once apparent, the saloon, nor is its chief object the promotion of temperance. It was not conceived in the belief that saloons are, in and of themselves, bad. It was not primarily concerned with that problem, for saloons were allowed on other days of the week. It was but one of several statutes, one prohibiting "sporting, rioting, quarreling, hunting, fishing, or shooting on Sunday," another "theatrical or dramatic performances," or "any equestrian

or circus performance of jugglers, acrobats, rope dancing, sparring exhibitions, variety shows, negro minstrelsy, living statuary, ballooning, or any baseball playing, or any ten pins, or other games of similar kind or kinds," another the engagement "in common labor" or the opening of "any building or place for the transaction of business," and still another providing a punishment for any one "who shall require any person in his employ or under his control to engage in common labor," on Sunday, and the only activities excepted are, according to the statute, "works of mercy or necessity," and, according to the courts, "intellectual labor,"—the latter exception, no doubt, more likely than the former, inspired by the lawyers. The basis of all this legislation was the contention that the Sabbath should be observed, and its object was to enforce the observance of the Sabbath, that is, to enforce an observance of the Sabbath in a certain way, devised by the Puritans, brought by them to this country, and handed down to and impressed upon their descendants. In any community composed of people

among whom the Puritan ideals and traditions prevail, the enforcement of such statutes was easy, because there was a general wish to observe them, and the other tendency was an exception; they represented the will of the people, they were in conformity with their customs and habits and employment, they were, in a word, law.

But America was not for the Puritans or their descendants alone, it was for all men, and there came here others, of a different tradition, of other, less severe, and in some respects, more cheerful ideals, people of different customs and habits and ways of viewing life. They wished to observe the Sabbath in a different manner. So here, a first difficulty arose. A second presents itself upon the appearance of another powerful factor, namely, the economic aspect which the problem assumes. In dealing with what are called moral problems, we are only beginning to take into consideration the influence of economic conditions in determining human conduct. This mode of observing the Sabbath, and the statutes enacted to enforce it found their rise

74

in purely agricultural communities. Men, accustomed to work out-of-doors all the week, coming at last wearily to a day of rest, were quite ready and willing to spend that day indoors. For rest, primarily, is change, and men who have been out-of-doors all week find a change within doors. Consequently the statutes relating to Sabbath observance were the more easily and readily accepted by the people, because, aside from any considerations of religion or piety, they were in conformity with their impulses, their desires, and their necessities. In the city, however, a different state exists. Here the conditions of employment are such that men, for the most part, are indoors all the week, and when the day of rest comes, they, or at least those to whom it does come, naturally as their country cousins went indoors, seek recreation in the open air. Again, when we reflect upon the intensity of the modern struggle for existence, the rigorous demands made upon the vital forces of men in the economic conflict, the long hours of toil in close and often ill-ventilated shops, stores and factories, the

nervous strain, the risk and danger in operating machines, it will be seen that some relaxation is necessary, and this fact, more than any other, explains the search for amusement, the theater, the ball game and all that. These things become a necessity under the economic conditions of to-day. The saloon, it is true, stands upon somewhat different grounds, yet, where the resort to it can not be explained on the ground of real or fancied social necessity, it being the only public place where many men may meet freely as equals and enjoy one another's society, it is found to be due to the necessity for stimulation decreed by this same insatiable machine, which, by hausting men's bodies in the mad greed for profits, drives them to stimulants in an impulsive effort to restore their wasted forces and exhausted bodies. And beyond all this, deeper, sadder, more pathetic far than all this, is the fact that thousands by society's grim machine are driven to drink by poverty, quite as often as they are driven to poverty by drink. Indeed, I think that Mr. Tom L. Johnson spoke the truth when he said "that there are more

people who drink because they are miserable, than there are people who are miserable because they drink."

The Sabbath realized by our Puritan ancestors has been altered by the conditions of our economic system. And if, as is often said and the fact deplored, the Sabbath has been destroyed it has been commercialism that has destroyed it. I have already tried broadly to indicate how the necessities of making a living under our present conditions have affected the customs and habits of men. Specific instances might be given which show how directly and positively the Sabbath has been wrested away from the people. It is a common thing in our cities to see large stores closed on Sunday, the curtains duly drawn, and the employees, some of them at least, thus granted a day of rest and recreation. But meanwhile all over the land there are freight trains running, and engineers, firemen, conductors, brakemen, switchmen, flagmen, despatchers, truckers, and numerous other employees, toiling long hours at hard and dangerous labor, to rush goods

77

to those emporiums by Monday morning. Now, it is not fair to lay the blame of this condition on the proprietors for they can not help it. They, like the men and women working for them, are in the grip of the commercial machine, and can not escape. All they can do is to use their undoubted influence to bring about conditions of toil less onerous to the masses, and, abandoning the efforts to have statutes passed and enforced to make men good by compelling them to observe the Sabbath, see to it that more fundamental statutes are so altered and amended that every man will have the same chance, the same opportunity, to be good that they have. Men can not be forced to be good, but they will become good if given the opportunity of enlightenment. I do not wish to be understood, in what I have here said, as saying that the Puritan method of observing the Sabbath is the correct one, or that it is not the correct one. How the Sabbath should be observed is, I think, a question that should be left to the individual conscience. I am speaking only of a fact, of a condition that does actually exist, here and every-

where. Nor do I wish to be understood, or represented, as advocating any kind of nullification of state statutes. I am simply trying to make clear the human obstacles to an absolute enforcement of all statutes that exist in these modern cities of ours.

There are on the statute books, federal, state and local, something like sixteen thousand statutes, and to enforce all of these, absolutely, all the time, is of course, to any mind but that of the theorist and the doctrinaire, absolutely impractical and impossible. An executive must do the best he can, with the means at his command, according to the light he has. In doing this, he can not, of course, satisfy all men; if he could be imagined as absolutely enforcing all these thousands of statutes all the time, he would satisfy no one, but succeed only in dissatisfying and provoking all, for at some time or another every man no doubt must violate some of these statutes, and as no man ever, under any possible circumstances, wishes the law enforced against him or his relatives or friends, it is clear that no man really believes that all laws should be enforced all the time.

Even you, in your suggestions as to more rigorous enforcement of the statutes relating to Sabbath observance, do not insist on the enforcement of them all. You select out of the number, but one, namely, that relating to the saloons. The others, those prohibiting baseball, for instance, or sporting, or other games, or keeping open stores, or the performance of or profiting by common labor, you omit. You do this, I venture to say, because you know from experience and observation, from your knowledge of men and of the world, and above all, from your perception and recognition of the custom and habits and necessities of the community, that their enforcement would be impractical, and indeed impossible, without bringing on tumult, and riot, and a whole train of evils much worse than the violation of these statutory regulations could possibly be. That is to say, you allow a certain discretion in the administration of these statutes, measured by the state of public sentiment and the degree of conformity thereto by custom. You come to the very point at which all who give deep consideration to the prob-

lem inevitably arrive, namely, that these statutes can be made applicable to human conduct, only in the way of auxiliary aids, they may guide it, to a degree regulate it, and perhaps educate and influence it, but they can never control it.

We had a striking illustration of this whole truth only recently when Judge Wachenheimer sought to enforce certain laws against certain citizens. Do you not remember the objection that was made, the outcry that was raised? And do you not remember that when Judge Wachenheimer came up for re-election he was defeated? This fact shows, I think, first, that all men do not believe in the enforcement of all laws all the time, and secondly, that a statute is not law merely because it is on the statute books. In the last few years, during a period of agitation and searching criticism, numerous efforts have been made by prosecutors to punish certain rich and respectable men for their violations of statutes, and yet, notwithstanding all the agitation, all the effort, here and all over the land, there are few instances, as far as I know, of a prosecutor who succeeded in

putting any of these men in prison, and not one single instance in which the people sustained him for doing so or for attempting to do so. It is undoubtedly not yet a custom for society to punish the acts which those statutes, that Wachenheimer, Heney and Folk and the other brave prosecutors sought to enforce, were enacted to punish, it is not a law; these acts are inextricably woven and interwoven into the fabric of our industrial system, they can not be separated from it, nor can their evils be avoided, until the whole fabric is renovated and renewed. And until that is done it will continue to be customary to maintain one law for the rich, and another for the poor, certain men will be let alone, and certain men punished, and until another ideal and another system shall prevail, courts and prosecutors will be powerless to convict. I would not have you understand me as wishing to see these men, or for that matter, any men, in prison; for my wish is the exact opposite to that. I do not pretend to judge men; I am not wise enough to know what justice is, in any case. I agree, indeed, with Mr.

OF LAW IN CITIES

William Dean Howells, in the belief that: "It seems best to be very careful how we try to do justice in this world, and mostly to leave retribution of all kinds to God, who really knows about things; and content ourselves as much as possible with mercy, whose mistakes are not so irreparable."

I say all this merely in the attempt to show you some of the difficulties of my position, some of the obstacles which an executive encounters, and to make clear how very difficult it is to give to a statute the vitality of a law unless the public sentiment, the custom and habit of the people, run in the same direction. And I seek also to make clear the further fact that to me it seems to be my duty to be guided by the will of the people of Toledo. The people elected me, I am responsible to them, and I have tried to be true to them. For me to employ force to combat their will would savor of tyranny, and I have neither the inclination nor the character of a tyrant.

In February, 1898, Samuel M. Jones was mayor of Toledo. Then as since, there was criticism of

the mayor; it was said by some that he did not enforce stringently enough the sumptuary laws. In order to test sentiment Mayor Jones ordered the most rigid enforcement possible of all the statutes and ordinances intended to compel Sunday observance. This was done for one, possibly two, Sundays. And this was the result: on the Monday evening following, namely, on the 14 February, 1898, the council, the direct representatives of the people, repealed every ordinance on the books of the city providing for Sabbath observance. Those ordinances have never been reenacted, and that vote is the last legally recorded and authoritative expression of the representatives of the people of this town on that subject.

I say that was the last expression of the people of this town on that subject. It was not, perhaps, strictly the last. Every time Mayor Jones ran for mayor, that issue was raised. Every time I have run, that issue has been raised. And every time that issue was raised Mayor Jones was reelected; every time that issue was raised, I have been elected.

Mayor Jones used to say that he thought he had fairly represented public sentiment in these matters, and fairly administered the law in accordance with that sentiment, and I think that I am perhaps fairly representing the will of the people, fairly administrating the law here.

The city, as we are slowly coming to understand, is an elemental thing. Its densely compacted masses take on some of the qualities of the hive, displaying vast inherent differences from scattered populations. The city has an individuality, a personality, and its unique conditions, employments, customs, habits, necessities, create a whole body of problems which demand distinct study and separate legislative treatment. While it has its part and its interest in the state, it nevertheless has problems of its own, and from the failure to recognize this fact, have arisen most of the conditions which cause many of us concern, and some, indeed, to despair. While humanity in the cities is not fundamentally different from humanity elsewhere, it has the especial needs of a different environment. The large

body of the laws and statutes have the same application, and find as ready observance in the city as elsewhere. But that different localities require different regulations in certain small respects, I think there is little doubt. We have had here, in our own town, in the instance I have just cited, an illustration of this. There is an adage to the effect that the way to repeal an obnoxious or unpopular law is to enforce it ruthlessly. This is so when those upon whom the obnoxious law is enforced, have the power, through representatives they themselves elect, to repeal it. When the case is otherwise, it is not so. The state legislature passes certain statutes that attempt to regulate the customs, diversions, sports and appetites of people in the cities. If rigorously enforced the people in the cities even if they desired, could not repeal them, for they are represented by a minority in the legislature. Each attempt of an executive to enforce those regulations would be met only by renewed applause from those who pass them and with whose habits of life they do not seriously interfere, but they would be intoler-

able to those upon whom their penalties were visited, those who had elected their executive to represent them, and not others. And many instances could be cited, in which city populations, resenting what to them savors of tyranny, have defeated administrations which were working out admitted reforms, of larger character and more fundamental significance. One of the cures for these ills, as I see it, is, first, to give the cities the power of local self government, or home rule, as it is usually called. Then the people of cities, in the regulation of their affairs, can on matters of purely local concern, make their own police regulations. This would insure a more positive and uniform observance of the law, and would do away with much of that disrespect of statutes which now exists.

The city must afford wider opportunity for rest and recreation; it must replace evil by substituting good, by providing wholesome, ennobling and elevating entertainment. A beginning has already been made in the parks, and to these should be added comfort stations, branch libraries,

band concerts and other music, public baths and swimming pools, playgrounds for the children and the grown-up alike, with ample opportunity for indoor and outdoor sports. The school buildings should be freely used by all the people, and noble public edifices should be erected, in which the people could take pride and delight. Then shall we have the beginnings of a healthy and an efficient democracy. And, of course, by methods of wider application, as I have said so often in these pages, we should do away with the causes of crime by an improvement in industrial and economic conditions. This can not be done by the mere enactment of statutes, but, perhaps slowly, gradually, by the discovery and application of juster principles, and by the upward urge of humanity as it becomes more enlightened, this great good may be brought to pass. The city is, indeed, the cradle of civilization. If it has shown humanity at its worst, it has also shown humanity at its best; if it has shown the lowest despair, it has also raised the highest hopes, and its contributions to science and literature and art have

been the most noble and brilliant achievements of men. It is to-day the hope of democracy, and if it be set free, I am sure that by the harmonious processes of liberty, it will become the triumph of democracy.

I am aware that this letter is already much too long. It has been written in those moments which I could find amid all the duties and the problems that daily perplex me. I have written in all kindness and in all sincerity. I respect your views and I sympathize with your aims for I know that you have no desire other than to make a city and a world better for men to dwell in. I have tried to make it clear that I desire no less than you, and according to the light that has been given me, I have tried to discharge my duties so that this good purpose may be advanced. This whole problem has been one to which I have given, I beg you to believe, not a little study. Looking out over the world, I have seen the sin, the poverty, the suffering, the shame of millions of wretched men and women, and little children, living in darkness and squalor, and vice and

crime, with no light, no hope, no joy in life, and the spectacle has been one inexpressibly sad. I have wondered how it all came about. I have struggled to comprehend it, sought to discover the cause of it. And I have tried to find some life concept, some light by which to be guided; and above all, something that I could do to make conditions a little better. Religion teaches that all men are the children of one common, all-loving Father, and therefore brothers; our nation has proclaimed to humanity in its fundamental law that all men are equal. And, as I have looked out upon the world, and witnessed the spectacle of misery, heard the long sad litany of human woe, I have seemed to see that it was all because we had lost faith in these precepts, that we are living lives, administering government, and all that, in a manner that traversed the claim of human brotherhood, and denied flatly the proposition of human equality. Looking more deeply, I have seen that our governments have abandoned the principle that all men are endowed with equal rights, and have adopted the theory that some are entitled to more

rights than others, and that accordingly, a few are to be selected and favored by privileges, and that all others are to be proscribed and compelled to toil, and to give the proceeds of their toil to the few privileged ones. As a result of all this, there have been idleness and viciousness and crime in the privileged, and those who have been proscribed and denied equal rights have been driven to poverty and hunger, and despair, and thence have come, naturally, logically, inevitably, vice and crime in them and their children. This condition is a blasphemous denial of religion; it is treason against our theory of government. And it has seemed to me that there was no other thing for me to do than to try, by the use of such poor powers and such small talents as I may possess, to aid and advance that cause which seeks to do away with privilege in the land, and to bring about equality and brotherhood. This is the oldest, as it is ever the newest, cause in the world. Those who have enlisted in it, even the most obscure of them, have found that it demands sacrifice, and yet those sacrifices or any sacrifices are im-

measurably outweighed by the consolations that come with the mere effort to serve humanity. They find, indeed, a greater solace and a greater satisfaction than any of which they had ever dreamed. Life has a new meaning, existence a nobler aim, for in this old cause men come into better and more beautiful relations with their fellow men, especially with those who are suffering and sinning in darkness and misery, and they can look forward with hope to that day when conditions will permit all men to live equal and brotherly and beautiful lives.

In this cause, the one for which all the sacrifices of the past have been made, the one in which all the long line of prophets and martyrs and poets have enlisted, the one in which the hope of the future rests, men learn a new philosophy. In that philosophy, all crime, all evil, all sin, are as abhorrent on Monday, or on any other day of the week, as on Sunday. They are abhorrent by whomsoever committed, whether rich or poor, high or low. Drunkenness, be it in a squalid or in a luxurious environment, is abhorrent to it. The prostitution of a man

92

who sells his talents as a lawyer, or preacher, or editor, or cartoonist, or speaker, to a cause in which privately he says he does not believe is found to be not only as bad as, but even worse than, that form which drives a girl into the street. Gambling remains gambling whether in a low den or a drawing-room, a swell club or a stock exchange, whether on a large or small scale, whether it be for pennies or for street-car franchises. In that philosophy, it is as great an offense to steal a railroad as it is to steal a ride, as great a crime to appropriate a coal mine as it is to pick up coal along the tracks; in that philosophy public property is as sacred as private property. And those committed to that philosophy are trying to put an end to these things, not by denouncing others who do them, but by trying to live lives that have no place for them, and by doing their utmost, in every relation of life, to stop them, and by doing away with the thing which very clearly is the cause of them, that is, Privilege.

That philosophy has no faith in the efficacy of force in making people good. It teaches that peo-

ple get better and improve, not by the destructive processes of hatred and wrath, but by the constructive method of love and reason. It teaches that goodness comes from within, not from without, that you can not beat goodness into people, or give them a prescription for it, to be taken in doses, like medicine, but that they must generate it out of their own hearts; and it believes that if we will only make social and economic conditions that will give all men, instead of a few men, a chance to live, they will naturally and inevitably become good. It teaches that you can not make people good by law, nor by policemen's clubs, nor by guns and bayonets, for it sees only hatred in these processes, and it knows that "hatred ceaseth not by hatred; hatred ceaseth but by love."

It discovered long ago that it is the inequality and the denial of brotherhood, resulting logically and inevitably from legal privilege, that make all the poverty, all the vice, all the crime in the world, the crimes of the poor and the crimes of the rich. This philosophy is one I am trying to apply in the

discharge of my duties. In doing so, I am being true to my own principles, true to my own conscience, true to "the light that lighteth every man that cometh into the world." And I hope that I may be given the strength to follow that light unto the end.

Sincerely yours,

BRAND WHITLOCK.

Toledo, 2 May, 1910.

Patterson Smith Reprint Series in
Criminology, Law Enforcement, and Social Problems

PATTERSON SMITH REPRINT SERIES IN
CRIMINOLOGY, LAW ENFORCEMENT, AND SOCIAL PROBLEMS